U. S. Supreme Court Decisions

51 Landmark Cases
Summarized and Explained
in Simple English

DOUGLAS MOSKOWITZ, Editor

This constitutional casebook is the outcome of the P.A.T.C.H. Law Program of the Northport–East Northport Union Free School District in New York. The casebook provides students and teachers with a summary review of 51 cases that support a better understanding of history and government.

A publication of Project P.A.T.C.H. of the Northport–East Northport U.F.S.D. and the Law Youth and Citizenship Program of the New York State Bar Association and State Education Department

© Copyright 1989
All rights are reserved, except that any part of this publication may be reproduced in any manner without the written permission of the publisher, provided that credit is given to the publisher for its availability.

ISBN: 978-1537637204

Reprinted 2016 by A. J. Cornell Publications

CONTENTS

5 Marbury v. Madison (1803)
6 McCulloch v. Maryland (1819)
7 Gibbons v. Odgen (1824)
8 Dred Scott v. Sanford (1857)
9 Ex parte Merryman (1861)
11 Munn v. Illinois (1877)
12 Santa Clara County v. Southern Pacific Railroad (1886)
13 Wabash, St. Louis & Pacific Railway Co. v. Illinois (1886)
14 Chae Chan Ping v. United States (1889)
16 Chicago, Milwaukee & St. Paul Railway Co. v. Minnesota (1890)
17 In re Debs (1895)
18 United States v. E. C. Knight Co. (1896)
19 Plessy v. Ferguson (1896)
20 Dorr v. United States (1904)
21 Lochner v. New York (1905)
22 Swift & Co. v. United States (1905)
23 Muller v. Oregon (1908)
24 Weeks v. United States (1914)
25 Hammer v. Dagenhart (1918)
26 Debs v. United States (1919)
27 Schenck v. United States (1919)
28 Schechter Poultry Corp. v. United States (1935)
30 West Virginia State Board of Education v. Barnette (1943)
31 Korematsu v. United States (1944)
32 Dennis v. United States (1951)
33 Brown v. Board of Education of Topeka (1954)
34 Watkins v. United States (1957)
35 Yates v. United States (1957)

36 Mapp v. Ohio (1961)
37 Engel v. Vitale (1962)
38 Abington School District v. Schempp (1963)
39 Gideon v. Wainwright (1963)
40 Escobedo v. Illinois (1964)
41 Heart of Atlanta Motel, Inc. v. United States (1964)
42 Miranda v. Arizona (1966)
43 Epperson v. Arkansas (1968)
45 Green v. County School Board of New Kent County, Va (1968)
46 Tinker v. Des Moines School District (1969)
47 Oregon v. Mitchell (1970)
48 New York Times Co. v. United States (1971)
49 P.A.R.C. v. Commonwealth of Pennsylvania (1971)
50 Swann v. Charlotte-Mechlenburg County Board of Education (1971)
51 Mills v. Board of Education of District of Columbia (1972)
52 Roe v. Wade (1973)
53 United States v. Nixon (1974)
54 Goss v. Lopez (1975)
56 University of California Regents v. Bakke (1978)
57 Board of Education, Island Trees School District v. Pico (1982)
59 New Jersey v. T.L.O. (1985)
60 Wallace v. Jaffree (1985)
61 Hazelwood School District v. Kuhlmeier (1988)

63 Appendix: Table of Cases, Organized by Major Ideas
68 Acknowledgments and Credits
70 Index

MARBURY v. MADISON (1803)

Concepts
Judicial v. Executive Power, Judicial Review

Facts
In his last few hours in office, President John Adams made a series of "midnight appointments" to fill as many government posts as possible with Federalists. One of these appointments was William Marbury as a federal justice of the peace. However, Thomas Jefferson took over as President before the appointment was officially given to Marbury. Jefferson, an Anti-Federalist, instructed Secretary of State James Madison not to deliver the appointment. Marbury sued Madison to get the appointment he felt he deserved. He asked the Court to issue a *writ of mandamus*, requiring Madison to deliver the appointment. The Judiciary Act, passed by Congress in 1789, permitted the Supreme Court of the United States to issue such a writ.

Issue
Whether the Supreme Court of the United States has the power, under Article III, Section 2, of the Constitution, to interpret the constitutionality of a law or statute passed by Congress.

Opinion
The Court decided that Marbury's request for a *writ of mandamus* was based on a law passed by Congress that the Court held to be unconstitutional. The Court decided unanimously that the federal law contradicted the Constitution, and since the Constitution is the Supreme Law of the Land, it must reign supreme. Through this case, Chief Justice John Marshall established the power

of judicial review: the power of the Court not only to interpret the constitutionality of a law or statute but also to carry out the process and enforce its decision.

This case is the Court's first elaborate statement of its power of judicial review. In language that remains relevant today, Chief Justice Marshall said, "It is emphatically the province and duty of the judicial department to say what the law is." Nowhere in the Constitution does the Court have the power that Chief Justice Marshall proclaimed. Despite there being no mention of such power in the Constitution, since 1803, our Nation has assumed the two chief principles of this case: that when there is a conflict between the Constitution and a federal or state law, the Constitution is supreme; and that it is the job of the Court to interpret the laws of the United States.

McCULLOCH v. MARYLAND (1819)

Concepts
"Necessary & Proper" Clause, Federal Supremacy v. State Rights

Facts
The state of Maryland brought an action against James William McCulloch, a cashier in the Maryland branch of the Bank of the United States, for not paying a tax the state had imposed on the United States Bank.

Issue
Whether the state of Maryland had the right to tax a federal agency that was properly set up by the United States Congress.

Opinion
In a unanimous decision, the Supreme Court of the United States ruled that the "power to tax involves the power to destroy," and that the federal government's national bank was immune to state taxation. The Court reasoned that Congress could set up a United States Bank and write laws "necessary and proper" to carry out its constitutional power to coin and regulate money.

GIBBONS v. OGDEN (1824)

Concepts
Interstate Commerce, Federal Supremacy v. State Rights

Facts
Robert Livingston secured from the New York State Legislature an exclusive twenty-year grant to navigate the rivers and other waters of the State. The grant further provided that no one should be allowed to navigate New York waters by steam without a license from Livingston and his partner, Robert Fulton, and any unlicensed vessel should be forfeited to them. Ogden had secured a license for steam navigation from Fulton and Livingston. Gibbons originally had been partners with Odgen but was now his rival. Gibbons was operating steamboats between New York and New Jersey under the authority of a license obtained from the United States. Ogden petitioned the New York court and obtained an injunction ordering Gibbons to stop operating his boats in New York waters.

Issue
Whether the New York statute that prohibited vessels

licensed by the United States from navigating the waters of New York was unconstitutional and, therefore, void.

Opinion
Writing for the Supreme Court of the United States, Justice Marshall said that the injunction against Gibbons was invalid because the monopoly granted by the New York statute conflicted with a valid federal law. The Court used this case to put forth the position that Congress can legislate and regulate all matters of interstate commerce as long as there is some commercial connection with another state. While interstate commerce is regulated by Congress, power to regulate "completely internal" commerce (trade carried on in a state that does not affect other states) is reserved to the states.

DRED SCOTT v. SANFORD (1857)

Concepts
Slavery, Question of Citizenship v. Fifth Amendment, Property Rights

Facts
Dred Scott, a slave, was taken by his owner, Sanford, into northern federal territory. Scott felt that he was free because of the *Missouri Compromise of 1820,* which excluded slavery from specified portions of United States territories. When he came back to Missouri, Scott sued his owner for his freedom.

Issue
Whether Dred Scott, a slave, was a citizen of the United States and legally entitled to use the courts to sue.

Opinion
The Supreme Court of the United States ruled that slaves were property, not citizens, and, therefore, Dred Scott was not entitled to use the courts. The Court focused on the rights of the owner, not the slave, saying that black people had no rights that white people were bound to respect. Justice Taney said that freeing Scott would be a clear violation of the Fifth Amendment because it would amount to depriving Sanford of his property without due process of law. He also said that Congress had no power to prohibit slavery in the territory and that the Missouri Compromise was unconstitutional.

[Justice Taney is considered one of the most prominent chief justices; however, *Dred Scott* has been widely criticized throughout history. Justice Taney believed that if he decided the case in favor of Scott, immediate civil war would have resulted. Associate Justice Curtis of Massachusetts, a liberal, disagreed so strongly with Taney's decision that he left the Court.]

EX PARTE MERRYMAN (1861)

Concepts
Writ of Habeas Corpus, Executive Power v. Civilian Due Process

Facts
John Merryman favored the South in the Civil War. A month after the war began in 1861, he was arrested and jailed for burning railroad bridges. His arrest was based on a vague suspicion of treason. There was no warrant issued, nor were there any witnesses nor proof of any

illegal action. Merryman wrote to Chief Justice Roger Taney, asking for a writ of habeas corpus so that his case would be tried in a civilian court. Chief Justice Taney issued the writ. However, the military commander in charge of Merryman's trial ignored the writ, citing President Lincoln's suspension of habeas corpus in certain parts of the country.

Issue
Whether the President of the United States has the power to suspend a writ of habeas corpus without the consent of Congress, and whether Merryman was deprived of life, liberty, or property without due process.

Opinion
Chief Justice Taney, who was holding circuit court (which Supreme Court justices did then), challenged President Lincoln's suspension of the writ of habeas corpus. The Chief Justice believed that the President drew too much power for himself without the consent of Congress. He criticized the President for improperly substituting military authority for civilian authority and emphatically warned that the people of the United States were "no longer living under a government of laws, but . . . at the will and pleasure of the army officer in whose military district they happen to be found."

[Eventually, Merryman was handed over to civilian authorities, and Congress gave the President the power, which he had previously drawn to himself, to suspend the privilege of habeas corpus at his discretion during wartime.]

MUNN v. ILLINOIS (1877)

Concepts
Public-Private Property, Free Enterprise v. State Rights

Facts
Midwestern farmers felt that they were being victimized by the exorbitant freight rates they were forced to pay to the powerful railroad companies. As a result, the state of Illinois passed a law that allowed the state to fix maximum rates that railroads and grain elevator companies could charge.

Issue
Whether the regulation of railroad rates by the state of Illinois deprived the railroad companies of property without due process of law.

Opinion
The Supreme Court of the United States upheld the Illinois law because the movement and storage of grain were considered to be closely related to public interest. This type of economic activity could be governed by state legislatures, whereas purely private contracts could be governed only by the courts. The Court held that laws affecting public interest could be made or changed by state legislatures without interference from the courts. The Court said, "For protection against abuse by legislatures, the people must resort to the polls, not the courts."

SANTA CLARA COUNTY v. SOUTHERN PACIFIC RAILROAD (1886)

Concepts
Corporate Tax, State Power to Tax v. Equal Protection

Facts
Santa Clara County taxed the Southern Pacific Railroad. However, the corporation refused to pay the taxes, claiming that the taxes were assessed at the full monetary value without the discount that was given to individual property owners for extremely large mortgages. The Southern Pacific claimed that under the Fourteenth Amendment, their corporation, which should be treated as an individual, was denied equal protection under the law.

Issue
Whether corporations should be treated as individuals under the Fourteenth Amendment, and whether the state of California denied Southern Pacific Railroad equal protection under the law.

Opinion
The Supreme Court of the United States agreed with the railroad and upheld the lower court decision that Santa Clara County wrongfully taxed the Southern Pacific Railroad. Under the Fourteenth Amendment of the Constitution, corporations are treated as individuals; therefore, their taxes should be assessed at a smaller value, the same way it is done for individual property owners.

[This case is often cited in other cases because it stands for the principle that the word *person* in the Fourteenth Amendment applies to corporations as well as natural persons and both are entitled to the equal protection of the laws under the Constitution, Thus, corporations are now considered legal persons and can sue and be sued.]

WABASH, ST. LOUIS & PACIFIC RAILWAY CO. v. ILLINOIS (1886)

Concepts
Individual Property Rights v. State Rights, Commerce Clause

Facts
An Illinois statute imposed a penalty on railroads that charged the same or more money for passengers or freight shipped for shorter distances than for longer distances. The railroad in this case charged more for goods shipped from Gilman, Illinois, to New York, than from Peoria, Illinois, to New York, when Oilman was eighty-six miles closer to New York than Peoria, The intent of the statute was to avoid discrimination against small towns not served by competing railroad lines and was applied to the intrastate (within one state) portion of an interstate (two or more states) journey.

Issue
Whether a state government has the power to regulate railroad prices on that portion of an interstate journey that lies within its borders.

Opinion
The Supreme Court of the United States held the Illinois statute to be invalid and that the power to regulate interstate railroad rates is a federal power which belongs exclusively to Congress and, therefore, cannot be exercised by individual states. The Court said the right of continuous transportation from one end of the country to the other is essential and that states should not be permitted to impose restraints on the freedom of commerce. In this decision, the Court gave great strength to the commerce clause of the Constitution by saying that states cannot impose regulations concerning price, compensation, taxation, or any other restrictive regulation interfering with or seriously affecting interstate commerce.

[One year after *Wabash*, Congress enacted the Interstate Commerce Commission (ICC). This commission had the power to regulate interstate commerce.]

CHAE CHAN PING v. UNITED STATES (1889)

Concepts
Treaties, Congressional Powers, Immigration

Facts
Between 1848, when gold was discovered in California, and the time of this case, the number of Chinese laborers in the United States greatly increased. During this short time, the Chinese immigrant population grew to become seventeen percent of the California population. This threatened American workers' jobs, forcing Con-

gress to pass the Chinese Exclusion Act of 1882. The Act permitted the United States to regulate the flow of Chinese immigrants into the United States. Chae Chan Ping, a subject of the Emperor of China and a laborer by trade, lived in San Francisco, California. He left for China in 1875, but was not allowed to return to the United States in 1888 because of the new legislation. Ping contended that the Act violated existing treaties with China and that he should be allowed to re-enter the United States.

Issue
Whether an act of Congress that excluded Chinese laborers from the United States was a constitutional exercise of congressional power even though the act conflicted with an existing treaty with China.

Opinion
The Supreme Court of the United States ruled that Congress did have the right to deny Chae Chan Ping's re-entry into the United States. Saying that treaties are equivalent to acts of Congress and can be repealed or amended, the Court reasoned that it was permissible to exclude the Chinese because the preservation of independence and the security against foreign aggression are the highest duties of every nation. All other considerations are subordinate. Congress must have the power to do whatever it may deem essential in order to maintain and protect the United States. Such power includes the control over the immigration of aliens and their return to the United States. The Court decided that Congress had the authority to determine whether certain foreigners should be excluded.

CHICAGO, MILWAUKEE & ST. PAUL RAILWAY CO. v. STATE OF MINNESOTA (1890)

Concepts
Railroad Rates, Procedural Due Process v. State Rights

Facts
In 1887 the state of Minnesota passed an act to regulate common carriers (i.e., railroads). The act declared that any unreasonable charge for service in the transportation of passengers or property was to be unlawful and prohibited. Certain trade unions complained that the Chicago, Milwaukee and St. Paul Railway charged some shippers up to four cents per gallon for the transportation of milk. They believed that these prices were unreasonable and unlawful under the act.

Issue
Whether states have the authority to regulate the rates railroads charge for transportation of passengers or goods.

Opinion
The Supreme Court of the United States invalidated the Minnesota law because it authorized administrative rate-making without providing for judicial review (a hearing). The Court held that the state of Minnesota has the power to regulate and question the reasonableness of rates; however, the railroads were entitled to more procedural protection. The Court upheld the state railway commission's right to regulate railroad rates but the commission had to give the railroads an opportunity to question and be heard if the rates established by the

commission were unreasonable.

IN RE DEBS (1895)

Concepts
Union Strikes, Commerce Clause v. First & Fourteenth Amendments

Facts
Eugene V. Debs, an American railway union officer and one of the leaders of the Pullman Railroad Car workers' strike in 1894, refused to honor a federal court injunction ordering him to halt the strike. Debs appealed his contempt of court conviction.

Issue
Whether the federal government has the constitutional authority to stop railroad workers from striking.

Opinion
The Supreme Court of the United States, in a unanimous decision, upheld the authority of the federal government to halt the strike. The Court reasoned that the federal government has "enumerated powers" found in Article 1, Section 8, to "regulate commerce ... among the several states," and to establish post offices and post roads. When the American Railway Union struck, it interfered with the railroad's ability to carry commerce and mail, which benefited the needs and "general welfare" of all Americans.

UNITED STATES v. E. C. KNIGHT CO. (1895)

Concepts
Anti Trust Acts, Congressional Power v. Free Enterprise

Facts
The Sherman Anti-Trust Act, passed by Congress in 1890, was an attempt to limit the growth of corporate power. Prior to this case, the American Sugar Refining Co., through stockholder agreements, purchased stock in smaller companies and eventually controlled 90 percent of the sugar processed in the United States. The federal government regarded the acquisition of the sugar refining companies as an illegal restraint of interstate commerce.

Issue
Whether Congress has the authority to regulate manufacturing, and whether the Sherman Anti-Trust Act outlawed manufacturing monopolies.

Opinion
The Supreme Court of the United States believed that there were certain aspects of economic life that should be regulated by the federal government and other aspects that should be left to the states to regulate. Here, where the federal government sued under the Sherman Act to break up the large sugar refining monopoly of Knight, the Court held that the federal government could not regulate refineries since they were "manufacturing operations" that were not directly related to interstate commerce. The Court reasoned that the states,

under the Tenth Amendment, should have the right reserved to them to regulate "local activities," such as manufacturing.

[In subsequent cases, the Court modified its position and permitted Congress greater regulation of commerce.]

PLESSY v. FERGUSON (1896)

Concepts
Separate But Equal, Equal Protection v. State Rights

Facts
In 1892 Plessy purchased a first-class ticket on the East Louisiana Railway, from New Orleans to Covington. Louisiana. Plessy, who was of racially mixed descent (one-eighth black and seven-eighths Caucasian), was a United States citizen and a resident of the state of Louisiana. When he entered the train, he took a seat in the coach where only whites were permitted to sit. He was told by the conductor to leave the coach and to find another seat on the train where non-whites were permitted to sit. Plessy did not move and was ejected with force from the train. Plessy was sent to jail for violating the Louisiana Act of 1890, which required railway companies to provide "separate but equal" accommodations for white and black races. Plessy argued that this law was unconstitutional.

Issue
Whether laws that provided for these separation of races violated the rights of blacks as guaranteed by the equal protection clause of the Fourteenth Amendment.

Opinion
The Supreme Court of the United States held that the Louisiana Act, which stated that "all railway companies were to provide equal but separate accommodations for white and black races" did not violate the Constitution. This law did not take away from the federal authority to regulate interstate commerce, nor did it violate the Thirteenth Amendment, which abolished slavery. Additionally the law did not violate the Fourteenth Amendment, which gave all blacks citizenship, and forbade states from passing any laws which would deprive blacks their constitutional rights. The Court believed that "separate but equal" was the most reasonable approach considering the social prejudices that prevailed at the time.

[The Plessy doctrine of "separate but equal" was overturned by *Brown v. Board of Education of Topeka* (1954), which held "separate but equal" to be unconstitutional.]

DORR v. UNITED STATES (1904)

Concepts
Jury Trial, Rights of the Accused v. Congressional Power over Territories

Facts
After the Spanish-American War in 1898, the United States obtained the Philippines, Cuba, Guam, and Puerto Rico as territories. In the Philippines, Dorr was arrested for libel. Dorr was editor of the *Manila Freedom,* a radical newspaper opposing the government. Denied a trial by jury, he lost his case and appealed to the Supreme Court of the United States, claiming that his constitutional right to a trial by jury had been denied.

Issue
Whether a trial by jury is necessary in a judicial proceeding in the Philippine Islands where the accused person has been denied a jury trial.

Opinion
The Court ruled that a trial by jury in the Philippines, or in any other United States territory, is not a "constitutional necessity," and the conviction was upheld. The Court concluded that the Constitution gives Congress the power to acquire and govern new territory but does not provide for the right of trial by jury in those territories. However, Congress could pass a law requiring trial by jury in the territories. The territorial government of the Philippines did not have to provide a jury trial in criminal cases unless Congress passed legislation requiring it to do so.

LOCHNER v. NEW YORK (1905)

Concepts
Work Hours Per Week, Individual Property Rights v. State "Police Powers"

Facts
A New York law set limits on how many hours bakery employees could work. Lochner was convicted and fined fifty dollars for permitting an employee to work more than the lawful number of hours in one week. On appeal, Lochner claimed that the New York law infringed on his right to make employer/employee contracts.

Issue
Whether a law that limited the number of hours bakery employees were allowed to work interfered with the bakery owner's right to make employer/employee contracts.

Opinion
The Supreme Court of the United States held that even though states have the power to regulate in the areas of health, safety, morals, and public welfare, the New York law in question was not within the limits of these "police powers" of the State.

[This decision marked the beginning of the "substantive due process" era, in which the Court struck down a number of state laws that interfered with an individual's economic and property rights. It was overturned twelve years later in *Bunting v. Oregon* (1917).]

SWIFT v. UNITED STATES (1905)

Concepts
Price Fixing, Free Enterprise v. Congressional Power

Facts
Under various congressional anti-trust acts, Congress had the power to prevent price fixing and monopolies. Swift and other meatpackers arranged to fix or alter the price of livestock bought and sold in Chicago, in violation of these acts. Swift argued that it was not involved in interstate commerce since the stockyard transactions were the middle part of the meatpacking process and took place only within the state.

Issue
Whether the Sherman Anti-Trust Act could bar price fixing by meat dealers within a state.

Opinion
The Supreme Court of the United States held that although the price fixing related to stockyard activities that occurred in one state, they were a part of a "stream of interstate commerce" and, therefore, could be regulated by the federal government under the commerce clause of the United States Constitution.

MULLER v. OREGON (1908)

Concepts
Employee-Employer Contracts, Tenth Amendment v. Fourteenth Amendment

Facts
In 1903 the state of Oregon passed a law prohibiting women from working in factories or laundries more than ten hours in any day. In 1905 a suit was filed against Curt Muller for making Mrs. E. Gotcher work more than ten hours in one day. Found guilty, Muller took his case to the Supreme Court of the United States, charging that he was wrongly convicted because the legislation of the state of Oregon was unconstitutional. He believed that his Fourteenth Amendment rights were infringed upon by his inability to make his own hours for his employees.

Issue
Whether the state of Oregon, through its regulation of women's work hours, violated the "privileges and im-

munities" clause of the Fourteenth Amendment by forbidding the employment of women for more than ten hours a day in laundries and factories.

Opinion
The Court held that the Oregon law that barred women (who were viewed as a weaker class and in need of special protection) from certain factory and laundry work to be correct and sustained the legislation. The Court distinguished the *Lochner* case, where an employer's "liberty to contract" outweighed the state's interest to regulate bakery employees' hours, from this case, which took into account the physical differences between men and women. The Court took judicial notice (based upon a famous brief submitted by then-lawyer, Louis D. Brandeis) of the belief that "women's physical structure and the function she performs . . . justify special legislation restricting the conditions under which she should be permitted to toil."

WEEKS v. UNITED STATES (1914)

Concepts
Search and Seizure, "Police Powers," Exclusionary Rule

Facts
Fremont Weeks was suspected of using the mail system to distribute chances in a lottery, which was considered gambling and was illegal in Missouri. Federal agents entered his house, searched his room, and obtained papers belonging to him. Later, the federal agents returned to the house in order to collect more evidence and took letters and envelopes from Weeks' drawers. In both instances, the police did not have a search warrant. The

materials were used against Weeks at his trial and he was convicted.

Issue
Whether the retention of Weeks' property and its admission in evidence against him violated his Fourth Amendment right to be secure from unreasonable search and seizure and his Fifth Amendment right not to be a witness against himself.

Opinion
The Supreme Court of the United States unanimously decided that as a defendant in a criminal case, Weeks had a right to be free from unreasonable search and seizure and that the police unlawfully searched for, seized, and retained Weeks' letters. The Court praised the police officials for trying to bring guilty people to punishment but said that the police could not be aided by sacrificing the fundamental rights secured and guaranteed by the Constitution.

[This decision gave rise to the "Exclusionary Rule." This meant that evidence seized in violation of the Constitution cannot be admitted during a trial.]

HAMMER v. DAGENHART (1918)

Concepts
Child Labor, Congressional Powers v. State Rights, Commerce Clause

Facts
In 1916 Congress passed the Child Labor Law, which prohibited the interstate transportation of products

made by companies that employed young children who worked long hours.

Issue
Whether congressional powers under the commerce clause extended far enough to prohibit the interstate transportation of products made in factories in which underage children worked.

Opinion
In a 5-4 decision, the Supreme Court of the United States held that the Child Labor Law of 1916 was unconstitutional. The Court reasoned that Congress was trying to regulate child labor laws by using the commerce clause and that the employment of children was not directly related to interstate commerce. The Court felt that Congress should not impinge upon the states' right to oversee child labor by using its power to regulate commerce so as to indirectly regulate child labor.

DEBS v. UNITED STATES (1919)

Concepts
Clear and Present Danger, Free Speech v. Congressional War Powers

Facts
Eugene V. Debs, a well-known socialist, gave a public speech to an assembly of people in Canton, Ohio. The speech was about the growth of socialism and contained statements which were intended to interfere with recruiting and advocated insubordination, disloyalty and mutiny in the armed forces. Debs was arrested and charged with violating the Espionage Act of 1917.

Issue
Whether the United States violated the right of freedom of speech given to Debs in the First Amendment of the United States Constitution.

Opinion
The Supreme Court of the United States upheld the lower court's decision in favor of the United States. The Court said that Debs had actually planned to discourage people from enlisting in the Armed Forces. The Court refused to grant him protection under the First Amendment freedom of speech clause, stating that Debs "used words [in his speech] with the purpose of obstructing the recruiting service." Debs' conviction under the Espionage Act would stand, because his speech represented a "clear and present danger" to the safety of the United States.

SCHENCK v. UNITED STATES (1919)

Concepts
Clear and Present Danger, Free Speech v. Congressional War Powers

Facts
Charles T. Schenck and Elizabeth Baer, charged with conspiring to print and circulate documents intended to cause insubordination within the military, were convicted of violating the Espionage Act of 1917 The act made it a crime to "willfully cause or attempt to cause insubordination, disloyalty, mutiny, or refusal of duty in the military ... or to willfully obstruct the recruiting service of the United States." Schenck appealed the conviction to the Supreme Court of the United States,

claiming all his actions were protected by the First Amendment.

Issue
Whether Schenck's and Baer's First Amendment right to freedom of speech were violated when they were convicted of conspiring to obstruct the recruitment and enlistment of service.

Opinion
The Court unanimously upheld the conviction of Schenck, not for violation of the Espionage Act, but rather for conspiracy to violate it. The Court found that the First Amendment did not apply in this else, and that Schenck's speech was not constitutionally protected because it posed a "clear and present danger" to the country. The nation was involved in World War I, and the Court saw Schenck's speech and action as counterproductive to the national war effort. The Court reasoned that certain speech could be curtailed, using the example of a situation where one cannot yell "fire" in a crowded theatre.

SCHECHTER POULTRY CORP. v. UNITED STATES (1935)

Concepts
Congressional Power v. Presidential Power, Commerce Clause, "Sick Chickens"

Facts
During the Great Depression, President Franklin Delano Roosevelt established an economic recovery pro-

gram known as the "New Deal." As part of the program, the President established the National Industrial Recovery Act of 1933 (NIRA), which authorized the President to set "codes of fair competition," regulating certain facets of interstate commerce. The Schechter Poultry Corp. bought, slaughtered, and sold chickens only in New York State, although some of the chickens were purchased from other states. Schechter was indicted for disobeying the "live poultry code," one of the codes of fair competition. The government alleged that Schechter failed to observe minimum wage and hour provisions, permitted customers to select individual chickens from particular coops and half-coops, sold unfit and uninspected chickens, and made false reports. Schechter appealed his conviction.

Issue

Whether the National Industrial Recovery Act, which gave the President the authority to regulate certain aspects of commerce during the Depression, was an unconstitutional delegation of presidential power.

Opinion

The Supreme Court of the United States, in a unanimous decision, held that the delegation of power made by the NIRA was unconstitutional. The Court held that Congress has the power to regulate interstate commerce, not the President, and that Congress cannot delegate legislative power to the President. Even the extraordinary conditions of the Depression were not enough for the Court to allow the President to have more power than the Constitution gave him. Schechter's conviction was reversed because its business indirectly affected interstate commerce. The NIRA was declared unconstitutional because it exceeded the commerce power that had been given to Congress by the Constitution.

WEST VIRGINIA STATE BOARD OF EDUCATION v. BARNETTE (1943)

Concepts
Flag Salute, State Rights v. Establishment Clause

Facts
The West Virginia State Board of Education required by state law that all students salute the flag and recite the pledge of allegiance as a part of their daily routine. Students who refused were suspended, declared unlawfully absent, and subject to delinquency proceedings. Parents of such students were also subject to a fine or imprisonment. Several Jehovah's Witnesses, who were citizens of West Virginia, sought from the court an injunction to stop the West Virginia State Board of Education from requiring the pledge and flag salute.

Issue
Whether flag salute ceremonies in the schools violated students' liberties as guaranteed by the First Amendment.

Opinion
The Supreme Court of the United States ruled, 6-3, in favor of Barnette and the other Jehovah's Witnesses. The Court held that the Board of Education could not require daily flag salute and pledge as a condition that students must meet to receive a public education. The Court's ruling provided students "scrupulous protec-

tion" of their constitutional liberties as guaranteed by the First Amendment.

KOREMATSU v. UNITED STATES (1944)

Concepts
Japanese Relocation, Equal Protection v. Executive Powers

Facts
Between 1941 and 1945, there were strong anti-Japanese feelings in the United States due to the war with Japan. In May 1942, Korematsu, an American citizen of Japanese descent, was convicted in federal court of "knowingly remaining in a designated military area in San Leandro, California." His actions violated Exclusion Order #34 and Executive Order #9066 of 1942, which had been issued to protect the West Coast from acts of espionage and sabotage. The Acts required all Japanese-Americans living in restricted areas to go to inland relocation centers. Korematsu believed the order violated his constitutional rights.

Issue
Whether Executive Order #9066 of 1942, violated Korematsu's Fourteenth Amendment right to equal protection of the law and his Fifth Amendment right to life, liberty, and property; and whether, because of the special circumstance of the world war, Congress or the President had the power to violate Korematsu's constitutional rights.

Opinion
In a rare decision, 6-3, the Supreme Court of the United States ruled that an entire race could be labeled a "suspect classification," meaning that the government was permitted to deny the Japanese their constitutional rights because of military considerations. Because a number of Japanese may have been disloyal, the military felt that complete exclusion of persons of Japanese ancestry from certain areas was essential during wartime. The Court ruled that such exclusion was not beyond the war powers of Congress and the President since their interest in national security was "compelling."

DENNIS v. UNITED STATES (1951)

Concepts
Overthrow of Government, Free Speech v. National Security

Facts
Eugene Dennis was a leader of the Communist Party in the United States between 1945 and 1948. He was arrested in New York for violation of Section 3 of the "Smith Act." The Act prohibited advocation of the overthrow of the United States Government by force and violence. The government felt that the speeches made by Dennis presented a threat to national security. Dennis appealed his conviction to the Supreme Court of the United States, claiming that the Smith Act violated his First Amendment right to free speech.

Issue
Whether the Smith Act violated the First Amendment provision for freedom of speech or the Fifth Amend-

ment due process clause.

Opinion
The Court found that the Smith Act did not violate Dennis' First Amendment right to free speech. Although free speech is a guaranteed right, it is not unlimited. The right to free speech may be lifted if the speech presents a "clear and present danger" to overthrow any government in the United States by force or violence. Since the speech made by Dennis advocated his position that the government should be overthrown, it represented a "clear and present danger" to the national security of the United States.

BROWN v. BOARD OF EDUCATION OF TOPEKA (1954)

Concepts
School Segregation, Equal Protection v. State Rights

Facts
Four black children sought the aid of the courts to be admitted to the all-white public schools in their community after having been denied admission under laws that permitted racial segregation. The youths alleged that these laws deprived them of the equal protection of the law under the Fourteenth Amendment, even though their all-black schools were equal to the all-white schools with respect to buildings, curricula, qualifications and salaries of teachers, and other tangible factors.

Issue
Whether segregation of children in public schools de-

nies blacks their Fourteenth Amendment right of equal protection under the law.

Opinion
The Supreme Court of the United States looked not to the "tangible" factors but the effect of segregation itself on public education. The Court decided unanimously that segregation of black children in the public school system was a direct violation of the equal protection clause of the Fourteenth Amendment. It rejected the "separate but equal" doctrine of *Plessy v. Ferguson* (1896) and stated that this doctrine had no place in education. According to the Court, even if the facilities were physically equal, the children of the minority group would still receive an inferior education. Separate educational facilities were held to be "inherently unequal."

WATKINS v. UNITED STATES (1957)

Concepts
Self-incrimination, Un-American Activities, Right to Remain Silent v. Congressional Investigation

Facts
Watkins was convicted of violating a federal law that made it a crime for any person summoned as a witness by a congressional committee to refuse to answer any question asked by the committee. He had been summoned to testify before the House Committee on Un-American Activities. He testified about his own activities but refused to answer questions about whether other persons were members of the Communist Party. Watkins refused to answer the questions because he believed they were outside the scope of the Commit-

tee's activities and not relevant to its work.

Issue
Whether Watkins was within his rights to refuse to answer; and whether his conviction was a violation of the due process clause of the Fifth Amendment.

Opinion
The Supreme Court of the United States held that Watkins' conviction was invalid. The Court said that Congress had to spell out its purpose specifically to guarantee that people summoned to testify are treated fairly and given all their rights. The Court held that congressional committees are required to uphold the Bill of Rights and must grant citizens the freedom of speech. Such committees are restricted to the areas of investigation delegated to the committees, and no witness can be made to testify on matters outside those areas.

YATES v. UNITED STATES (1957)

Concepts
Communist Party, Free Speech v. Congressional Power

Facts
In 1951 fourteen persons were charged with violating the Smith Act for being members of the Communist Party in California. The Smith Act made it unlawful to advocate or organize the destruction or overthrow of any government in the United States by force. Yates claimed that his party was engaged in passive actions and that any violation of the Smith Act must involve active attempts to overthrow the government.

Issue
Whether Yates' First Amendment right to freedom of speech protected his advocating the forceful overthrow of the government.

Opinion
The Supreme Court of the United States said that for the Smith Act to be violated, people must be encouraged to do something, rather than merely to believe in something. The Court drew a distinction between a statement of an idea and the advocacy that a certain action be taken. The Court ruled that the Smith Act did not prohibit "advocacy of forcible overthrow of the government as an abstract doctrine." The convictions of the indicted members were reversed.

MAPP v. OHIO (1961)

Concepts
Warrantless Search, Right to Privacy v. State "Police Powers"

Facts
In May 1957, Cleveland police officers received a tip that Dollree Mapp was in possession of a large number of betting slips, and that a bomber was hiding in her home. When the police arrived at her house, Mapp refused to admit them without a search warrant. A few hours later, the police knocked again, then forcibly opened the door. A struggle ensued and Mapp was put in handcuffs, taken upstairs, and kept there while police searched her apartment. During the search, obscene materials were discovered in a trunk in her basement. Mapp was arrested for possession and control of ob-

scene materials.

Issue
Whether Mapp's Fourth Amendment right to be secure from search and seizure was violated during the search of her home.

Opinion
The Supreme Court of the United States ruled that Mapp's Fourth Amendment right to be secure from search and seizure was violated. The Court held that both the Fourth and Fourteenth Amendments protected persons from unwarranted federal and state intrusion of their private property.

ENGEL v. VITALE (1962)

Concepts
School Prayer, Establishment Clause v. State Rights

Facts
The Board of Education of New Hyde Park, New York, instructed the schools of their district to have students recite a NYS Regents–composed prayer at the beginning of each school day. Parents of a number of students challenged this policy. They said that the official prayer was contrary to their religious beliefs and that a governmental agency did not have the right to force prayer on students. The parents felt that the prayer violated the First Amendment's separation of church and state provision. The state contended that it was a non-denominational prayer and that the schools did not compel any student to recite it.

Issue
Whether a non-denominational prayer, recited in every classroom in a school district, violated the First Amendment's provision for separation of church and state.

Opinion
The Supreme Court of the United States found that the school district violated the students' First Amendment rights because even though the students did not have to say the prayer, the reciting of the prayer in class would put unwanted pressures on them. Further, this non-denominational prayer was found to be too religious for the state to mandate and was in violation of the establishment clause of the First Amendment.

ABINGTON SCHOOL DISTRICT v. SCHEMPP (1963)

Concepts
Bible Readings, Reserved Clause v. Establishment Clause

Facts
A Pennsylvania statute required that "at least ten verses from the Holy Bible shall be read at the opening of each public ... school day." A student could be excused from the Bible reading with a written note from a parent or guardian. The Schempp family, who had children in the Abington school system, disapproved of the Bible reading because it violated their religious beliefs. The family refused to write a letter to have their children excused, and took legal action to stop the school

district from conducting the daily Bible readings. The district court ruled in favor of the Schempp family. The school district appealed to the Supreme Court of the United States.

Issue
Whether a state, in creating a statute that promotes prayer in its public school system, is violating the establishment clause of the First Amendment, which states that the government may not establish any religion.

Opinion
The Court declared the law calling for "prayer in school" unconstitutional because it represented an establishment of religion by government. Stating that this was a direct violation of the establishment clause of the First Amendment, the Court prohibited Bible readings in public schools.

GIDEON v. WAINWRIGHT (1963)

Concepts
Right to Counsel, Rights of the Accused v. State Rights

Facts
Clarence Earl Gideon was arrested in 1961 and charged with breaking and entering a pool hall with intent to commit petty larceny (a felony). He did not have enough money for a lawyer and asked that one be appointed to defend him. The judge denied the request, saying that under Florida state law counsel can be appointed only in a capital offense. Gideon was sentenced to five years in prison He then filed a *writ of certiorari* (petition of appeal) to the Supreme Court of the United

States, asking for a case review. The Court granted Gideon's request and appointed Abe Fortas to represent him.

Issue
Whether the state of Florida violated Gideon's Sixth Amendment right to counsel, made applicable to the states by the Fourteenth Amendment, by not providing him with the assistance of counsel for his criminal defense.

Opinion
The Court ruled unanimously in Gideon's favor, and held that the Fourteenth Amendment included state as well as federal defendants. The Court said that all states must provide an attorney in all felony and capital cases for people who cannot afford one themselves. Through the Fourteenth Amendment due process clause, the Sixth Amendment guarantee of the right to counsel applies to the states.

[Gideon was retried in Florida and found not guilty.]

ESCOBEDO v. ILLINOIS (1964)

Concepts
Right to an Attorney, Self-Incrimination, Rights of the Accused v. State Rights

Facts
Danny Escobedo was arrested in 1960, in connection with the murder of his brother-in-law. After his arrest, he requested to see his lawyer but was not allowed to do so. After persistent questioning by the police, Escobedo

made a statement that was used against him at his trial, and he was convicted of murder. He appealed to the Illinois Supreme Court, which affirmed the conviction. Escobedo then appealed to the Supreme Court of the United States.

Issue
Whether the state of Illinois violated Escobedo's Fourteenth Amendment protections, his Fifth Amendment right to remain silent, and his Sixth Amendment right to assistance of counsel by denying his request to speak to a lawyer before questioning.

Opinion
The Court found that the denial by the police of Escobedo's right to counsel and their failure to inform him of his right to remain silent were clearly unconstitutional. Furthermore, the Court held that incriminating statements made by defendants are inadmissible as evidence unless the accused is informed of his rights before making the statements.

HEART OF ATLANTA MOTEL, INC. v. UNITED STATES (1964)

Concepts
Discrimination, Individual Property Rights v. Congressional Powers, Commerce Clause

Facts
The Civil Rights Act of 1964, passed by the United States Congress, prohibited racial discrimination and segregation in public accommodations. The owner of

the Heart of Atlanta Motel refused accommodations to blacks and filed suit, claiming that such control over an individual's business was not within the powers of Congress.

Issue
Whether the United States Congress, under its authority to regulate interstate commerce, has the power to require private businesses within a state to comply with the Civil Rights Act of 1964, which prevents discrimination in places of public accommodations.

Opinion
The Supreme Court of the United States held that the Civil Rights Act of 1964 was constitutional. The Court said that the commerce clause of the Constitution empowers Congress to regulate both commercial and noncommercial interstate travel. Since the motel served interstate travelers, its refusal to accommodate blacks posed a potential obstruction to their freedom of movement across state lines. Congress has a right to regulate individual businesses in the interest of promoting interstate travel.

MIRANDA v. ARIZONA (1966)

Concepts
Self-Incrimination, Rights of the Accused v. State "Police Powers"

Facts
Ernesto Miranda was convicted of rape and kidnapping. His conviction was based in part on incriminating statements he made to the police while they interro-

gated him. At no time during the questioning did the police inform Miranda that he did not have to talk to them or that he had the right to a lawyer when being questioned by police.

Issue
Whether the state of Arizona violated the constitutional rights of Miranda under the Fifth, Sixth, and Fourteenth Amendments when they interrogated him without advising him of his constitutional right to remain silent.

Opinion
The Supreme Court of the United States, in a 5-4 decision, ruled that the police were in error. The Court held that the police must inform suspects that they have the right to remain silent, that anything they say may be used against them, and that they have the right to counsel before the police may begin to question those held in custody.

[*Miranda* established the "Miranda Waning" which police now use prior to interrogation of persons arrested.]

EPPERSON v. ARKANSAS (1968)

Concepts
Teaching of Evolution, Establishment Clause v. State Rights

Facts
An Arkansas statute forbade teachers in public schools from teaching the "theory or doctrine that mankind ascended or descended from a lower order of animals." A teacher determined that the law was invalid and lost

her job for violating it. The Supreme Court of the United States was called in to review this statute, which made it unlawful for teachers in state schools to teach human evolution.

Issue
Whether the Arkansas statute that prohibited the teaching of evolution violated the establishment clause of the First Amendment and the equal protection clause of the Fourteenth Amendment of the Constitution because of its religious purpose.

Opinion
The Court held that the Arkansas statute forbidding the teaching of evolution in public learning institutions was contrary to the freedom of religion mandate of the First Amendment, and was also in violation of the Fourteenth Amendment. The Court ruled that a state may not eliminate ideas from a school's curricula solely because the ideas come in conflict with the beliefs of certain religious groups. In this case, the law that compelled the evolution doctrine to be removed from the course of study was passed to agree with the religious point-of-view of certain fundamentalists. Thus, the reason for removing the evolution doctrine was to aid a religious point-of-view and, therefore, was violative of the First Amendment. The Court said that the law must require religious neutrality.

GREEN v. COUNTY SCHOOL BOARD OF NEW KENT COUNTY, VA. (1968)

Concepts
Desegregation, Equal Protection v. State Rights

Facts
A small school district in Virginia, with two high schools and a fifty percent ratio black and white student population, adopted a "freedom of choice" plan whereby students could choose their own public school. Based on "free choice," black and white students segregated themselves. Calvin Green protested, claiming that the "freedom of choice" plan created a segregated school community instead of an integrated one.

Issue
Whether the district's "freedom of choice" plan, resulting in a segregated school community, violated the Fourteenth Amendment and the mandate of the Supreme Court of the United States established under the *Brown v. Board of Education of Topeka* (1954) decision.

Opinion
The Court unanimously decided in favor of Green. The Court noted that the first major school desegregation decision, *Brown*, held that segregated schools were inherently unequal. The Court held that the district's "freedom of choice" plan did not and would not bring about desegregation. The Court emphatically placed on the School Board of New Kent the burden of formulating a desegregation plan that would immediately and realistically achieve integration in its schools.

[*Green* is important because it set in motion the direction the federal district courts took during the 1970s in ordering busing and other affirmative desegregation steps so that a non-racial system of public education could be achieved.]

TINKER v. DES MOINES SCHOOL DISTRICT (1969)

Concepts
Symbolic Speech, Students' Right to Free Speech v. State Rights

Facts
In December 1965, Marybeth and John Tinker planned to wear black armbands to school, signifying their protest of the Vietnam War. School officials became aware of the plan beforehand and adopted regulation banning the wearing of such armbands. Failure to comply with this regulation would result in suspension until the student returned to school without the armbands. Both Tinkers went ahead and wore the black armbands to school. They were suspended and told not to return with the armbands. The Tinkers claimed that their rights of free speech and expression, which are protected under the First Amendment of the Constitution of the United States, had been violated, and that they should have been allowed to attend school wearing the armbands.

Issue
Whether the First Amendment's right to free speech grants Marybeth and John Tinker the right to wear

black armbands as a symbol of protest in a public school.

Opinion
The Court decided that the students did have a right to wear the armbands. It reasoned that the wearing of the armbands was an exercise of the students' right to free, silent, *symbolic* speech, which is protected under the First Amendment. "Students do not shed their constitutional rights at the schoolhouse gate, and therefore are entitled to the free expression of their views as long as there is no *substantial* or *material* interference of the educational process."

OREGON v. MITCHELL (1970)

Concepts
Right to Vote, State Rights v. Equal Protection

Facts
Several states challenged the Federal Voting Rights Act Amendments of 1970, which lowered the right to vote to age 18, expanded bans on literacy tests, and prohibited application of state durational residency requirements in presidential elections.

Issue
Whether Congress could grant 18-year-olds the right to vote in federal and state elections.

Opinion
The Court ruled to sustain the Voting Rights Act Amendments with respect to federal elections, but struck it down with respect to state elections.

[This decision was handed down on December 21,1970. Three months later, Congress submitted the Twenty-Sixth Amendment to the states for ratification. On June 30, 1971, the states ratified the Twenty-Sixth Amendment, which provided 18-year-olds the right to vote in all state and federal elections.]

NEW YORK TIMES CO. v. UNITED STATES (1971)

Concepts
Pentagon Papers, Free Press v. Executive Power

Facts
The United States wanted to restrain *The New York Times* and *The Washington Post* from publishing a classified study on Vietnam policy entitled "History of United States Decision-Making Process on Vietnam Policy," commonly called the "Pentagon Papers."

Issue
Whether the President of the United States had the power to stop the publication of historical news that might have an impact on the Vietnam War.

Opinion
The Supreme Court of the United States said that prior restraints (prohibiting information from being published or aired) are almost never valid. The Government must strongly justify any abridgment of a newspaper's freedom of speech. Since, in the eyes of the Court, national security was not threatened by the printing of the

"Pentagon Papers," no prior restraint was necessary and the Government's attempt at censorship was unconstitutional.

P.A.R.C. v. COMMONWEALTH OF PENNSYLVANIA (1971)

Concepts
Education for the Handicapped, Equal Protection v. State Rights

Facts
Several parents of mentally retarded children who were not getting an education brought a class action suit (under P.A.R.C.—the Pennsylvania Association for Retarded Children) on behalf of all mentally retarded persons who lived in Pennsylvania and who had been denied access to a free public education program appropriate to the individual student's capacity.

Issue
Whether the Commonwealth of Pennsylvania's denial of educational treatment for the mentally retarded violated the equal protection rights under the Fourteenth Amendment.

Opinion
The District Court found that mentally retarded persons are capable of benefiting from education and/or training. They can, with the state's help, achieve self-sufficiency or self care. Pennsylvania, having undertaken to provide a free education to all of its children, must provide mentally retarded children an educational pro-

gram that will meet their needs. Educational programs should take place, when possible, in a regular public school classroom.

SWANN v. CHARLOTTE-MECKLENBURG COUNTY BOARD OF EDUCATION (1971)

Concepts
Busing, School Desegregation

Facts
In *Brown v. Board of Education of Topeka* (1954), the Supreme Court of the United States ruled that racial segregation in public schools was unconstitutional. The *Swann* case [on behalf of six-year-old James Swann] deals with how school districts such as the Charlotte-Mecklenburg School District in North Carolina may restructure their attendance zones to comply with the Brown decision. The Charlotte-Mecklenburg Board of Education proposed a plan that involved busing students to balance the ratio of black to white students in its schools.

Issue
Whether forced busing and a restructured school system are methods of complying with the integration demands set forth in *Brown*.

Opinion
In a unanimous decision, the Court stated that changing attendance zones and busing students to various schools to create racial balance within the schools are

acceptable solutions to the problem of segregated school systems. Only when a child's health or education might be significantly hurt by busing should it be banned. The Court said that "a school district has broad powers to fashion a remedy that will assure a unitary school system."

MILLS v. BOARD OF EDUCATION OF DISTRICT OF COLUMBIA (1972)

Concept
Education for Exceptional Children, Equal Protection v. State Rights

Facts
Seven children of school age were denied education because they were mentally retarded, emotionally disturbed, hyperactive, or had behavioral problems. The Board of Education did not provide schooling for these exceptional children, violating controlling statutes and their own board regulations. It was also estimated that 18,000 similar "exceptional" children in the Washington, D.C., area were not in school. The D.C. school system admitted that it had failed its duty to provide these children with publicly supported education suited to their individual needs. It also had failed to provide prior hearings and periodic reviews of each exceptional student case.

Issue
Whether the Board of Education's failure to provide schooling, hearings, and periodic reviews for "exceptional" children violated the children's equal protection

and due process rights of the Fourteenth Amendment.

Opinion
The Supreme Court of the United States said that the Board of Education of the District of Columbia violated such rights as due process and certain statutes and regulations. The Court held that the Board of Education must provide public schooling for the exceptional children, along with a hearing beforehand to decide whether the child was exceptional. A plan was devised to adopt due process hearing procedures similar to that which the children requested. The Court said that the Board of Education had an obligation to provide whatever specialized instructions were needed to benefit the children, and that every child between the ages of seven and sixteen shall be provided regular instruction. No child eligible for public education should be excluded from school unless an adequate alternative suited to the child's needs was provided.

ROE v. WADE (1973)

Concepts
Abortion, Right of Privacy v. State Rights

Facts
A Texas woman [Norma Leah McCorvey, better known by the legal pseudonym "Jane Roe"] sought to terminate her pregnancy. However, a Texas law made it a crime to procure or attempt an abortion except when the mother's life would be in danger if she remained pregnant. Roe challenged the Texas law on the grounds that the law violated her right of personal liberty given in the Fourteenth Amendment and her right to privacy

protected by the Bill of Rights.

Issue

Whether state law that bans or regulates abortion violates a woman's right to privacy or personal choice in matters of family decisions or marriage.

Opinion

The Supreme Court of the United States decided that states could regulate abortions only in certain circumstances but otherwise women did have a right to privacy and reproductive autonomy. The Court divided a woman's pregnancy into three time periods: (1) during the first trimester (the first three months of pregnancy), states may not interfere with a woman's decision to have an abortion; (2) during the second trimester, states could regulate abortions, but only if such regulation was reasonably related to the mother's health; and (3) during the third trimester, which occurs after the fetus (unborn child) reaches viability (the stage at which it can survive outside the mother's body), states may regulate absolutely and ban abortions altogether in order to protect the unborn child. The woman's right to privacy was held to be a fundamental right that could be denied only if a compelling state interest existed. Once the fetus reaches a "viable" stage of development, such a compelling point is reached because the unborn child is now given constitutional protection.

UNITED STATES v. NIXON (1974)

Concepts

Watergate, Federal Due Process v. Executive Privilege

Facts
In the late 1970s, the Democratic National Headquarters at the Watergate Office Building in Washington, D.C. was broken into. The investigation that followed centered on staff members of then Republican President Richard M. Nixon. The Special Prosecutor subpoenaed certain tapes and documents of specific meetings held in the White House. The President's lawyer sought to deny the subpoena. The Special Prosecutor asked the Supreme Court of the United States to hear the case before the lower appeals court ruled on the President's appeal to deny the subpoena.

Issue
Whether the United States violated President Nixon's constitutional right of executive power, his need for confidentiality, his need to maintain the separation of powers, and his executive privilege to immunity from any court demands for information and evidence.

Opinion
By an 8-0 vote, the Court decided that President Nixon must hand over the specific tapes and documents to the Special Prosecutor. Presidential power is not above the law. It cannot protect evidence that may be used in a criminal trial.

GOSS v. LOPEZ (1975)

Concepts
Suspension, State Rights v. Students' Due Process

Facts
Several public high school students (including Dwight

Lopez) were suspended from school for misconduct but were not given a hearing immediately before or after their suspension. School authorities in Columbus, Ohio, claimed that a state law allowed them to suspend students for up to ten days without a hearing. The students brought a legal action, claiming that the statute was unconstitutional because it allowed school authorities to deprive students of their right to a hearing, violating the due process clause of the Fourteenth Amendment,

Issue
Whether the suspension of a student for a period of up to ten days without a hearing constitutes a violation of the due process clause of the Fourteenth Amendment.

Opinion
The Supreme Court of the United States said that education is a property interest protected by the Fourteenth Amendment's due process clause and any suspension requires prior notice and a hearing. Permitting suspension without a hearing is, therefore, unconstitutional. The Court said that oral or written notice of the charges brought against a student must be given to the student who is being suspended for more than a trivial period. If he denies the charges, the student must be given a hearing. The hearing may be an informal one, where the student is simply given an explanation of the evidence against him and an opportunity to tell his side of the story.

UNIVERSITY OF CALIFORNIA REGENTS v. BAKKE (1978)

Concepts
Affirmative Action, State Rights v. Equal Protection

Facts
Allan Bakke, a white male, applied to the University of California at Davis Medical School. He was denied admission because he did not meet the standard entrance requirements. Davis Medical School also had a special admissions program for minorities. Sixteen percent of the available places were reserved for minorities who did not meet the standard entrance requirements. Bakke argued that the requirements for special admissions to the medical school were discriminatory because only black, Chicane, and Asian students could compete for these places. The University of California argued that its special admissions program remedied the long-standing historical wrong of racial discrimination.

Issue
Whether the University's special admissions program, which accepted minority students with significantly lower scores than Bakke, violated Bakke's Fourteenth Amendment equal protection rights; and whether the University was permitted to take race into account as a factor in its future admissions decisions.

Opinion
The Supreme Court of the United States did not render a majority opinion in this case (i.e., one in which five or more of the nine justices agree). Six separate opinions were written, and no more than four justices agreed in

whole in their reasoning. The Court ordered Bakke's admission to Davis Medical School and invalidated the University's special admissions program because the program barred people like Bakke from applying for the special admissions seats in the medical school. However, of much greater significance was the fact that the Court allowed institutions of higher learning to take race into account as a factor in their future admissions decisions. Justices Brennan, White, Marshall, and Blackman said that this aspect was the central meaning of the case: "Government may take race into account when it acts not to insult any racial group but to remedy disadvantages cast on minorities by past racial prejudice."

[While to some observers Bakke won a place in the school and the particular special admissions program at Davis was invalidated, the case really stands as a landmark civil rights/affirmative action decision. Race may now be taken into account as a factor in college admissions.]

BOARD OF EDUCATION, ISLAND TREES SCHOOL DISTRICT v. PICO (1982)

Concepts
Book Banning, Reserved Clause v. First Amendment

Facts
The Board of Education of the Island Trees School District in New York directed the removal of nine books from the libraries of the Island Trees senior and

junior high schools because in the Board's opinion the books were "anti-American, anti-Christian, anti-Semitic, and just plain filthy." Some books included were *The Fixer, Soul on Ice, Slaughterhouse Five, Go Ask Alice, The Best Stories by Negro Writers,* and others. Four students from the high school and one from the junior high school sued the school district, claiming that the removal of the books was a violation of the First Amendment's guarantee of freedom of speech.

Issue
Whether the First Amendment limits a local school board's discretion to remove library books from senior and junior high school libraries.

Opinion
The Supreme Court of the United States ruled in favor of the students, saying that the books were not required reading. According to Justice Brennan, who cited *West Virginia Board of Education v. Barnette* (1943), "Local school boards may not remove books from school library shelves simply because they dislike the ideas contained in these books and seek by their removal to prescribe what shall be orthodox in politics, nationalism, religion, or other matters of opinion." He also cited *Tinker v. Des Moines School District* (1969), saying that high school students have First Amendment rights in the classroom. Although the schools have a right to determine the content of their libraries, they may not interfere with a student's right to learn. Therefore, the schools may not control their libraries in a manner that results in a narrow, partisan view of certain matters of opinion. The Court stood against the removal or suppression of ideas in schools.

NEW JERSEY v. T.L.O. (1985)

Concepts
Search and Seizure, State Rights v. Students' Due Process

Facts
In 1980 a teacher at Piscataway High School, New Jersey, discovered two girls smoking in the lavatory. Since smoking was a violation of a school rule, the two students—Tracy Lois Odem [referred to as "T.L.O."] and a companion—were taken to the principal's office. There they met with the assistant vice-principal who demanded to see T.L.O.'s purse. Upon opening the purse, he found cigarettes and cigarette rolling paper. He proceeded to look through the purse and found marijuana, a pipe, plastic bags, money, lists of names, and two letters that implicated her in drug dealing. T.L.O. argued the search of her purse was unconstitutional.

Issue
Whether the state of New Jersey and its agent, the assistant vice-principal, violated T.L.O.'s Fourth Amendment right of protection from "unreasonable search," her Fifth Amendment right of protection from self-incrimination, and her right to due process as provided in the Fourteenth Amendment.

Opinion
The Supreme Court of the United States held for the school and its assistant vice-principal. The Court reasoned that to maintain discipline in school, the school officials who have "reasonable suspicion" that a student has done something wrong can conduct a reasonable

search of the suspicious student. A school's main objective is to educate students in a legal, safe learning environment. Police need "probable cause," a higher standard, to search people, places, and things. School officials, unlike the police, need only "reasonable suspicion" to search students when they believe unlawful conduct is occurring.

WALLACE v. JAFFREE (1985)

Concepts
Moment of Silence, State Rights v. Establishment Clause

Facts
The parents of three children attending public school in Alabama challenged the constitutionality of an Alabama law that authorized a one-minute period of silence in all public schools for meditation or voluntary prayer.

Issue
Whether the Alabama law requiring a one-minute silence period encouraged a religious activity in violation of the First Amendment establishment clause.

Opinion
The Supreme Court of the United States held that the Alabama law was a law respecting the establishment of religion and thus violated the First Amendment. The Court said that the First Amendment was adopted to limit the power of Congress to interfere with a person's freedom to believe, worship, and express himself as his conscience tells him. The Amendment gives an individual the right to choose a religion without having to ac-

cept a religion established by the majority or by government.

The Court said that government must be completely neutral toward religion and not endorse any religion. Therefore, statutes like the Alabama law requiring one minute for silence in the schools must have a secular or non-religious purpose to be within the Constitution. Since State Senator Donald G. Holmes, who was the primary sponsor of the bill, testified "that the bill was an effort to return voluntary prayer to our public schools," the Court decided that the purpose of the Alabama law was to endorse religion and was solely an effort to return voluntary prayer to the public schools. It was, therefore, struck down as being inconsistent with the Constitution.

HAZELWOOD SCHOOL DISTRICT v. KUHLMEIER (1988)

Concepts
Censorship, State Rights v. Students' Free Press Rights

Facts
Kathy Kuhlmeier and two other journalism students wrote articles on pregnancy and divorce for their school newspaper. Their teacher submitted page proofs to the principal for approval. The principal objected to the articles because he felt that the students described in the article on pregnancy, although not named, could be identified, and the father discussed in the article on divorce was not allowed to respond to the derogatory article. The principal also said that the language used

was not appropriate for younger students. When the newspaper was printed, two pages containing the articles in question as well as four other articles approved by the principal were deleted.

Issue

Whether the Hazelwood School District violated the freedom of expression right of the First Amendment by regulating the content of its school newspaper.

Opinion

The Supreme Court of the United States held that the Hazelwood School District did not violate the First Amendment right of the students. The Court ruled that although schools may not limit the personal expression of students that happens to occur on school grounds, *Tinker v. Des Moines* (1969), they do not have to promote student speech that they do not agree with. This decision gave schools the power to censor activities such as school plays and school newspapers as long as the school finances the activities and there are grounds for the censorship. The Court said in *Tinker* that in order to censor a student's expression, the expression must substantially disrupt the school's educational process, or impinge upon the rights of others. This case broadened that guideline to include censorship of unprofessional, ungrammatical, or obscene speech, or speech that goes against the fundamental purpose of a school.

APPENDIX: TABLE OF CASES, ORGANIZED BY MAJOR IDEAS

(Prepared by Sandy Scarpinito, "American History Through Constitutional Law" Instructor)

AGRARIAN PROTEST
Munn v. Illinois (1877)
Wabash. St. Louis & Pacific Railway Co. v. Illinois (1886)
Chicago, Milwaukee & St. Paul Railway Co. v. Minnesota (1890)

ANTI-TRUST
Munn v. Illinois (1877)
United States v. E. C. Knight Co. (1895)
Swift & Co. v. United States (1905)

AVENUE OF REPRESENTATION
Oregon v. Mitchell (1970)

CHILD LABOR
Hammer v. Dagenhart (1918)

CIVIL LIBERTIES
Weeks v. United Slates (1914)
Mapp v. Ohio (1961)

CIVIL RIGHTS
Brown v. Board of Education of Topeka (1954)

COLD WAR
Dennis v. United States (1951)
Watkins v. United States (1957)
Yates v. United States (1957)

CONTROVERSY / NEW DEAL
Schechter Poultry Corp. v. United States (1935)

CORPOATE v. INDIVIDUAL RIGHTS
Lochner v. New York (1905)
Muller v. Oregon (1908)
Hammer v. Dagenhart (1918)

CRIMINAL LIBERTIES
Gideon v. Wainwright (1963)
Escobedo v. Illinois (1964)
Miranda v. Arizona (1966)

DECISIONS ON CIVIL RIGHTS SINCE 1948
Heart of Atlanta Motel, Inc. v. United States (1964)
Green v. County School Board of New Kent County, Va. (1968)
Swann v. Charlotte-Mechlenburg County Board of Education (1971)
University of California Regents v. Bakke (1978)

DECLARATION OF INDEPENDENCE
Dorr v. United States (1904)

DEMOCRACY: ITS RIGHTS AND FREEDOMS
Marbury v. Madison (1803)
West Virginia State Board of Education v. Barnette (1943)
Engel v. Vitale (1962)
Abington School District v. Schempp (1963)
Epperson v. Arkansas (1968)
Wallace v. Jaffree (1985)

EQUALITY
Plessy v. Ferguson (1896)
Brown v. Board of Education of Topeka (1954)
Swann v. Charlotte-Mechlenburg County Board of Education (1971)
University of California Regents v. Bakke (1978)

NATIONAL GOVERNMENT / RESPONSE / ICC
Gibbons v. Odgen (1824)
United States v. E. C. Knight Co. (1895)
In re Debs (1895)
Schechter Poultry Corp. v. United States (1935)

NIXON AS PRESIDENT
Oregon v. Mitchell (1970)

PRESIDENTIAL POWERS
Korematsu v. United States (1944)
United States v. Nixon (1974)

PROPERTY RIGHTS
Munn v. Illinois (1877)

RAILROAD POOLING / RATES
Wabash. St. Louis & Pacific Railway Co. v. Illinois (1886)

REACTION TO IMMIGRATION
Chae Chan Ping v. United States (1889)

RIGHTS OF THE DISABLED
P.A.R.C. v. Commonwealth of Pennsylvania (1971)
Mills v. Board of Education of District of Columbia (1972)

RIGHTS OF ETHNIC/RACIAL GROUPS
Dred Scott v. Sanford (1857)
Chae Chan Ping v. United States (1889)

RIGHTS OF WOMEN
Roe v. Wade (1973)

SCIENCE AND RELIGION
Epperson v. Arkansas (1968)

SEGREGATION
Plessy v. Ferguson (1896)
Brown v. Board of Education of Topeka (1954)

SEPARATE BUT EQUAL
Plessy v. Ferguson (1896)
Brown v. Board of Education of Topeka (1954)

SOCIAL ISSUES / MODERN TIMES
Roe v. Wade (1973)
Goss v. Lopez (1975)
Board of Education, Island Trees School District v. Pico (1982)
New Jersey v. T.L.O. (1985)
Wallace v. Jaffree (1985)
Hazelwood School District v. Kuhlmeier (1988)

SPANISH-AMERICAN WAR
Dorr v. United States (1904)

STATES RIGHTS v. FEDERAL SUPREMACY
McCulloch v. Maryland (1819)
Gibbons v. Odgen (1824)

STUDENT PROTESTS / VIETNAM
Tinker v. Des Moines School District (1969)
New York Times Co. v. United States (1971)

SUPREME COURT INTERPRETATION OF THE 14TH AMENDMENT
Munn v. Illinois (1877)
Santa Clara County v. Southern Pacific Railroad (1886)
Lochner v. New York (1905)
Muller v. Oregon (1908)

WAR IMPACT ON MINORITIES
Korematsu v. United States (1944)

WARTIME CONSTITUTIONAL ISSUES
Debs v. United States (1919)
Schenck v. United States (1919)
Korematsu v. United States (1944)

WARTIME MEASURES
Ex parte Merryman (1861)
Schenck v. United States (1919)
Korematsu v. United States (1944)

WATERGATE
United States v. Nixon (1974)

ACKNOWLEDGMENTS

This project will remain a memorable experience for many "American History Through Constitutional Law" students. The project was made possible because of their enthusiasm and dedication. They spent hundreds of hours bringing this guide together. I would like to thank my fellow classmates who negotiated, researched, developed, wrote, typed, and edited the fifty-one Supreme Court case summaries in the text. I would also like to thank:

The Northport–East Northport Union Free School District, and its law program. Project P.A.T.C.H., and the New York State Bar Association and its Law, Youth & Citizenship Program, for sponsoring this project.

The P.A.T.C.H. teaching staff, who guided all our efforts, especially Sandy Scarpinito and William Perilli.

Peter C. White, Esq., our legal scholar, who reviewed our work.

Dr. Eric S. Mondschein, Director of Law, Youth & Citizenship, who promoted and supported this project.

Mr. Thomas J. O'Donnell, Director of Project P.A.T.C.H., for his support and assistance.

Mr. William Martin, who found us space and time in the computer room.

Mr. Richard Knoeppel and Mrs. Helen LoCurto for their assistance in preparing the materials for publication.

A Very Special Thank You to my classmate, Jason Scurti, for his support, assistance, and editorial skills which brought the whole project together.

—*Douglas Moskowitz, Editor-in-Chief*

CREDITS

Editor-in-Chief: Douglas Moskowitz

Associate Editor-in-Chief: Jason Scurti

Student Negotiating Team: Jennifer Bies, Lawrence Finn, Brian Murtagh, Kristen McQuillian, Robert Peters

Legal Scholar: Peter C. White, Esq.

Project P.A.T.C.H. Director: Thomas J. O'Donnell

Law, Youth & Citizenship Program Director: Dr. Eric S. Mondschein

American History Through Constitutional Law Instructors: William Perilli, Sandy Scarpinito, Peter Stachecki

INDEX

38 Abington School District v. Schempp (1963)
57 Board of Education, Island Trees School District v. Pico (1982)
33 Brown v. Board of Education of Topeka (1954)
14 Chae Chan Ping v. United States (1889)
16 Chicago, Milwaukee & St. Paul Railway Co. v. Minnesota (1890)
26 Debs v. United States (1919)
32 Dennis v. United States (1951)
20 Dorr v. United States (1904)
 8 Dred Scott v. Sanford (1857)
37 Engel v. Vitale (1962)
43 Epperson v. Arkansas (1968)
40 Escobedo v. Illinois (1964)
 9 Ex parte Merryman (1861)
 7 Gibbons v. Odgen (1824)
39 Gideon v. Wainwright (1963)
54 Goss v. Lopez (1975)
45 Green v. County School Board of New Kent County, Va. (1968)
25 Hammer v. Dagenhart (1918)
61 Hazelwood School District v. Kuhlmeier (1988)
41 Heart of Atlanta Motel, Inc. v. United States (1964)
17 In re Debs (1895)
31 Korematsu v. United States (1944)
21 Lochner v. New York (1905)
36 Mapp v. Ohio (1961)
 5 Marbury v. Madison (1803)
 6 McCulloch v. Maryland (1819)
51 Mills v. Board of Education of District of Columbia (1972)
42 Miranda v. Arizona (1966)
23 Muller v. Oregon (1908)

11 Munn v. Illinois (1877)
59 New Jersey v. T.L.O. (1985)
48 New York Times Co. v. United States (1971)
47 Oregon v. Mitchell (1970)
49 P.A.R.C. v. Commonwealth of Pennsylvania (1971)
19 Plessy v. Ferguson (1896)
52 Roe v. Wade (1973)
12 Santa Clara County v. Southern Pacific Railroad (1886)
28 Schechter Poultry Corp. v. United States (1935)
27 Schenck v. United States (1919)
50 Swann v. Charlotte-Mechlenburg County Board of Education (1971)
22 Swift & Co. v. United States (1905)
46 Tinker v. Des Moines School District (1969)
18 United States v. E. C. Knight Co. (1895)
53 United States v. Nixon (1974)
56 University of California Regents v. Bakke (1978)
13 Wabash, St. Louis & Pacific Railway Co. v. Illinois (1886)
60 Wallace v. Jaffree (1985)
34 Watkins v. United States (1957)
24 Weeks v. United Slates (1914)
30 West Virginia State Board of Education v. Barnette (1943)
35 Yates v. United States (1957)

www.ingramcontent.com/pod-product-compliance
Lightning Source LLC
Chambersburg PA
CBHW071838200526
45169CB00020B/1847